Praise for *Persp*...

"This highly readable volume discu... ...ector development in Uganda. The style is highly refreshing. The chapters are both technically professional, and address and often challenge accepted wisdoms, but the account is also personal and colored by the first-hand experiences of a highly motivated young professional working alongside the Ugandan central bank as a Fellow of the Overseas Development Institute (ODI). This demonstrates the huge value of this well-esteemed program in fostering the enthusiasm and commitment of talented young professionals. True credit to Prajakta for assembling the lessons from her exposure to the Ugandan environment! Much can be learnt from the understanding, commitment and advice provided in this volume both as regards the development of financial systems in Uganda, in other countries in Africa and elsewhere."

- **MICHAEL FUCHS**, retired as Advisor, Finance and Private Sector Development, The World Bank. Led ten Financial Sector Assessment Programs (FSAPs) in Sub-Saharan Africa between 2002-2013, including Nigeria (2012), and a 5-country FSAP for the East African Community (2013)

"This is a fascinating first-hand account of the experience of a young Indian economist trained at the London School of Economics, placed at the Bank of Uganda as an ODI fellow. It captures very well the tension between received knowledge and the challenge of policymaking and between being an expert and learning from the real world. The account of this intellectual journey would interest anyone interested in or involved with development policy."

- **MAITREESH GHATAK**, Professor and Deputy Head of the Economics Dept., London School of Economics and Political Science

"The ideas in Perspectives on Uganda are in a way a reflection of the issues that Prajakta considered very important in her daily work. Indeed, this book is a reflection of how deeply involved she had become with Ugandan issues. True to her views, she advocated home grown solutions to regulatory issues. She argues that the policy tool kit for prudential authorities in economies such as Uganda should be a mix of home-grown solutions and international best practices adapted to the local context. You will find in this book a reasonable balance in an otherwise broad mix of themes that range from finance, accountability and tax avoidance to the role of Chinese development aid. I am delighted to recommend Perspectives on Uganda to anyone interested in issues affecting the country's current development path and those that are shaping its future. I also commend it to anyone with an interest in African development more broadly. These are my personal views and not for the Bank of Uganda and do not in any way commit Bank of Uganda as an organisation."

- **MRS. JUSTINE BAGYENDA**, Executive Director of Supervision, Bank of Uganda

"'Perspectives on Uganda' is a refreshing read for anyone who wishes to delve into what it is like to live in Uganda. It sheds light on some fascinating and some funny aspects of the situation in the country, be it economic development, mobile innovations or rural credit co-operatives. As someone who came in close contact with the Ugandan authorities and people through my work, I would strongly recommend reading this compilation of first-hand reflections"

- **MIQUEL DIJKMAN**, Senior Financial Sector Specialist, The World Bank

"Mrs. Prajakta Kharkar Nigam is very passionate about her work and the people around her. This is reflected in the essays that she has put together – they are a result of her interactions with Ugandans of all walks of life. This book tackles a number of very important themes that are currently very topical in Uganda. These include the challenges facing the nascent financial sector, the innovations in the payments system as well as the regulation of SACCO'S. These are all critical policy issues for the country and its people. Indeed, as someone who was closely involved in the setting up of the nascent Financial Stability Department at the Bank of Uganda – readers will find her discussion of these critical issues very informative. This book leads me to believe that a lot must be written about Uganda for the benefit of the future generations. I hope that her effort will open the way for the dissemination to wider audiences of some of the challenges that policy makers in developing countries face in reforming their financial sectors. I recommend this Book to everyone who is interested in the improvement of the quality of the day-to-day life of the ordinary people in developing countries."

- **CHARLES AUGUSTINE ABUKA**, Director, Financial Stability Department, Bank of Uganda

Perspectives on Uganda
Reflections of an ODI Fellow

Copyright © Prajakta Kharkar Nigam, 2016

ISBN #: 978-1-365-33144-2

All rights reserved.

For Baba, on your 60th birthday— I hope this will qualify for a place in your personal library, which I have revered since I was a child.

Table of Contents

Acknowledgements 2

Foreword 4

Introduction 7

Towards Accountability 9

Uganda's Financial Sector at 50: Challenges and Innovation 15

Financial Stability in Uganda: Much Ado About Nothing? 27

Innovation in Payment Systems 41

Chinese Development Aid to Uganda 53

Tax Avoidance in Uganda 61

Regulation Not a Panacea for SACCO Troubles 69

Enhancing Uganda's Business Competitiveness 77

Acknowledgements

This book would have been impossible without encouragement and support from my husband, Shashank Nigam, the relentless follow-up by my parents, Prashant Kharkar and Gauri Kharkar, and the delightful presence of my daughter Sanaa.

These essays have benefited from my interactions with several people in Uganda, some pursuing coveted careers in important positions, others doing common jobs in the homes of expatriates and on the streets of Kampala. I thank my friend Aaron Timothy Kirunda, who introduced me to Uganda and her heritage beads for the very first time in 2007. At that time, I had no clue I would spend two years living in Uganda later on. Much perspective has also come from my day-to-day observation of life while working at Bank of Uganda (BOU) with colleagues, many of whom became great friends and a periscope into the life of the locals. I am grateful to my mentors at Bank of Uganda, particularly Deputy Governor Dr. Louis Kasekende, Executive Director of Supervision Mrs. Justine Bagyenda and Director of Financial Stability Department Dr. Charles Abuka, whose guidance was invaluable time and again in understanding their country.

Dinner-table discussions with the Overseas Development Institute (ODI) Fellows, fellowship alumni, and visiting experts from international organizations and the expatriate community in Kampala have been most insightful and often added spark to my curiosity. I owe special thanks to friends I've made in the Indian community in Uganda, who have become family forever.

I thank my editor Barbara McNichol, whose patience and excellent editing were critical in clarifying my messages. Last, but not the least, I thank my early supporters who pre-ordered copies of this book through my Publishizer campaign – Anna Solé Amat, Astrid Haas, Christine van Hooft, Dhawal Kulkarni, Dileep Nigam, Guy Vincent, Kshitija Raje, Kunal Varty, Madhuri Kulkarni, Manali Mandrekar, Neha Kulkarni, Paritosh Kharkar, Vijeta Sawant, Peter Richens, Renuka Iyer, Prashant Kharkar, Shashank Nigam and Dr. Hemant Joshi.

All the views expressed in this book and any errors or omissions herein are my own and do not represent the views of any of my advisors, colleagues, or employers in the past or present.

Foreword

Africa is a diverse continent, a fertile ground for opening the eyes of a young economist to the complex economic, social, and anthropological processes that have shaped the continent. This book looks at some such interesting characteristics of Uganda from the lens of a bold yet thoughtful economist.

Prajakta was posted to Bank of Uganda as an economist for two years as part of the Overseas Development Institute (ODI) Fellowship Scheme. Funded by the Department for International Development (UK), this is a prestigious fellowship programme well known over half a century for its rigorous selection process and deep in-country engagement with government ministries and central banks in nearly 50 countries. This opportunity placed Prajakta at the heart of several financial-sector policy matters in Uganda—a great vantage point to come face to face with the dilemmas of the day in the country.

As an economist and policymaker, I found the perspectives that this book offers on multiple aspects of Uganda refreshing. Through my various roles at the World Bank, African Development Bank, and Bank of Uganda over the past three decades, it has become clear that we need home-grown solutions to Africa's challenges. Some of the articles in the book echo this eloquently.

Written with the sharp analytical edge of an economist and the youthful inquisitiveness of an explorer, the essays in this book serve to intrigue as much as enlighten. Prajakta raises questions that are pertinent and sometimes hidden in plain sight of policy practitioners. She critically re-examines various business practices and re-awakens civic consciousness about several policy choices in Uganda. More importantly, the essays shed light on Prajakta's personal experience in Uganda and some of her interactions at the Central Bank. These add depth and authenticity to her writing, distinguishing it from both, detached academic research and sensational journalism.

I am pleased to recommend this book of essays to anyone who wishes to make acquaintance with the economic and social issues in Uganda for work, for travel, or for intellectual discovery.

Louis Kasekende, Ph.D.

Deputy Governor of the Bank of Uganda

Introduction

Uganda is an unforgettable place, blessed with refreshing natural beauty but scarred by its past and entangled in its socio-economic peculiarities. The country has a way of preserving a child-like optimism for her future in the hearts of her people. Most Ugandans I met seemed happy and hopeful, be it a high-ranking officer in the government, a businessman, or a *boda-boda* driver on the streets of Kampala. This both surprised and disoriented me because I'd been sent to this "developing country" as an "expert" to build capacity. I had come to work for the central bank, Bank of Uganda, as an ODI Fellow. However, living and working in Uganda for two years led to an important realisation: I have much to see and learn here. The terminology we use to describe the stages and aspects of economic development is often too simplistic and narrow to categorise the condition of African societies and economies.

Ugandan society amused me, enraged me, bewildered me, and humbled me. Living there taught me patience and the ability to appreciate diversity of perspectives on the very definition of progress. It reinforced some of my beliefs and overturned others. I wrote these essays during the course of my stay in Uganda as a way to distil my thoughts on these observations.

Uganda is a rich and complex environment. This compilation is in no way a comprehensive picture of life and the state of affairs in Uganda. My aim is to provide a flavour for the social and business landscape of Uganda by sharing my personal reflections over two years I spent in the country, with anyone wishing to explore this place – an Overseas Development Institute Fellow, a development economist, a humanitarian worker, a researcher, a traveller or even a Ugandan wishing to see her country through a different lens.

Uganda is fascinating to the explorer, humbling to the critic, and captivating to anyone who comes to Uganda with an open mind. One can't help but want to return to this place. I hope this book will provide an easy way for me and any interested readers to do so. In a way, I am inviting you on my time machine.

Welcome on board!

Towards Accountability

In 2012, a large-scale corruption scam in the Office of the Prime Minister (OPM) of Uganda was uncovered. The OPM staff had allegedly embezzled aid for reconstruction in the northern Ugandan region—a region that had been ravaged by civil war for 20 years. Atrocities by Joseph Kony's Lord's Resistance Army (LRA) rebels had displaced more than two million people internally and killed thousands.

When peace began to be restored in 2008, donor agencies decided to provide *direct* budget support to the government of Uganda to rehabilitate this region. However, in 2012, the Office of the Auditor General of Uganda reported that USD 14.4 million given as aid had been embezzled.[1] This sparked strong reactions from both the international donor community and the civil society in Uganda.

In response, donor countries including the U.K., Ireland, Germany, Austria, Belgium, Sweden, Denmark, and Norway suspended up to USD 300 million promised in budget support each

---

[1] The Foreigner. "Norway demands Uganda Aid Refund" (http://theforeigner.no/pages/news/norway-demands-uganda-aid-refund/)

year.[2] The suspension would last until 2013 *or* until Uganda's government took stringent measures to control corruption. That would include bringing corrupt civil servants to task. *This marked one of the most serious actions taken collectively by the donors against corruption.*

As a saving grace, the misuse of funds was uncovered during Uganda's domestic audit. Eventually, George Kazinda, the OPM's principal accountant at the time of this alleged embezzlement, was found guilty and sentenced to five years imprisonment.

However, public sentiment following this verdict suggested that people did *not* believe a scam of such magnitude could have been accomplished by one individual. And if it had been—considering the large number of Northern Ugandan people who were deprived of basic amenities without these funds—his sentence seemed too lenient.

However, it's disappointing that the tone of local media coverage suggests that Uganda has now seen how suddenly aid flows could stop, so we need to make this economy self-reliant. Good lesson to take but not the *right* one. Nearly a quarter of Uganda's national budget is funded by direct budget support from donor countries. I don't think the cuts in aid indicate any change in

---

[2] Dear Jeanne and John Njoroge, *Daily Monitor*. December 4, 2012. "Donors cut all direct aid to government until 2013"

(http://www.monitor.co.ug/News/National/Donors++cut++all+direct+aid++government++until+2015/-/688334/1635792/-/a1433q/-/index.html)

the donors' commitment to development in Africa. Instead, these cuts are aimed at sending a signal to recipient countries.

The point is, the international community takes corruption, embezzlement of development funds, war crimes, and human rights violations seriously—more so than political leaders in recipient countries would like to believe. Even if economies in the African continent wean themselves off aid in the future (which I pray they do), the arsenal of measures against regimes engaging in such unacceptable behaviour would anything but shrink.

While aid should not be used to arm-twist any country into accepting conditions that hurt its progress, doing away with dependence on foreign aid cannot be expected to silence the world on ethical violations. Being economically self-reliant doesn't come with a license to engage in malpractices without questioning.

If not those in the international community, then the citizens themselves will question the regimes and topple them if necessary— as happened during the Arab Spring uprisings of 2012. These revolutions, which started in Tunisia, swept across Arab nations. People took to the streets in protest against oppressive leadership and eventually even toppled the regimes in several places.

African economies that have been poster children for foreign aid are not immune to international backlash if unacceptable practices such as corruption continue. Any aid cuts are intended to lead to improving governance in African regimes. Economic self-reliance that comes with discipline and accountability is welcome but intended as only a side benefit.

Moreover, I think Uganda's budgeting process in 2013 emphasized the immense difficulty of suddenly weaning the country off foreign budget support. Whether direct budget support is an effective tool for development is a different debate altogether. However, given that Uganda has been receiving substantial amounts of aid in this form, the country has indeed become over-reliant on it in several key areas of public expenditures. Self-reliance won't happen overnight, and if it does come too quickly, it will come at too high a price to the average taxpayer. Therefore, the Ugandan government needs to take measured steps to improve accountability and rebuild its relationship with donors.

In response to the aid suspension, Uganda's 2013 budget included tax increases on certain key amenities and services. While this may be argued as a painful but necessary step to help the economy in becoming self-reliant, in practice, I doubt if government leaders had the time or luxury to respond in any other way. The aid suspension was simply too sudden and unexpected. As a result, greater tax revenues were the quickest short-term source of funding needed public expenditures.

However, this event shouldn't be used as an excuse for a long-term contractionary fiscal policy. Continued heavy taxation would severely hurt the citizens' standard of living. After all, who actually pays for the consequences of aid suspension? The common people, who are vulnerable to the slightest fall in disposable income.

In the long run, such suffering gets compensated at the aggregate level. Yet, at the individual level, personal well-being declines and, unfortunately for the poorest of the poor, it often happened more than proportionately.

A better but less palatable alternative to taxation is available to Uganda. The tax increases in the 2013 budget may have been inevitable. In the future, however, concrete steps to bring transparency and accountability into Uganda's systems could make donor countries consider reinstating their budget support. Prioritising cleaning up of the systems so relationships with donors can be revived is crucial. That way, Uganda could still reduce its reliance on aid but at a slower pace with minimal damage to its citizens' incomes and well-being.

While Uganda faces the risk of crucial budget support being withdrawn indefinitely, the government's inaction to salvage this support and the media's tone suggest government leaders don't even recognise how critical it is for Uganda.

Note on recent developments: This article was originally published online on the blog Africa at LSE in April 2013. As of November 2015, the Ugandan government has repaid part of the embezzled aid money to some donor countries. The enactment of the Public Finance Management Act 2015 and the creation of a single treasuries account are also steps towards greater accountability. Yet, the challenge lies in the effective enforcement of such laws. Direct budget support from Britain, a key donor for Uganda, still remains suspended indefinitely.

Uganda's Financial Sector at 50: Challenges and Innovation

When Uganda became independent in 1962, only four commercial banks existed in the country—Standard Chartered, Barclays, Grindlays, and Bank of Baroda. These banks concentrated on mobilising deposits and offering short-term loans to finance foreign trade and provide working capital, mainly to foreign companies and non-residents.

Then the government of Uganda established two public banks, the Uganda Commercial Bank and the Cooperative Bank. These banks primarily provided inclusive banking services, especially credit. For two and a half decades after independence, the financial sector was largely driven by the state. Its financial services comprised a limited array of products: savings accounts, current accounts, and fixed deposit accounts. It primarily served as a conduit for financing national economic development initiatives.

While economic development was no doubt a priority for the government, the financial sector was operating with little regard for market dynamics, best practices, or prudential regulations. By the late 1980s, widespread impairment of loan portfolios and financial repression plagued the system. For the masses, access to the financial system was minimal.

Reforms Brought Stability

The reforms of 1990s brought about the liberalisation of state controls over the financial sector and specifically the abolishment of interest rate and credit controls. Along with that, prudential regulation of the financial sector began to receive attention. The intent? Protect the interests of depositors and build confidence in financial services while maintaining the soundness and stability of the system. Key legal milestones included the enactment of the Financial Institutions Statute (FIS) in 1993 and the Financial Institutions Act a decade later in 2004. During this period, the Central Bank—Bank of Uganda (BOU)—took over several insolvent or mismanaged banks. This resulted in considerable recovery of the Ugandan financial sector during the decades that followed.

The financial sector in Uganda now consists of commercial banks, credit institutions, micro-deposit-taking institutions, payment platforms, insurance companies, brokerage and investment management companies, and the Uganda Securities Exchange. Of these, the commercial banking industry is the largest component, with 25 licensed banks and the National Social Security Fund (NSSF) accounting for nearly 80% of the financial sector's assets. The Ugandan banking industry shows signs of better market practices, buffers of capital above the statutory minimum, low levels of impaired credit, and strong profitability.

Challenges and Emerging Innovations

However, against a backdrop of growth and cleansing, the market mechanism in Uganda's financial sector remains imperfect. Much needed innovative solutions that go beyond the banking industry are emerging to address them. Three are discussed here.

Affordability of Credit: Under Bank of Uganda's inflation-targeting framework, the Central Bank Rate (CBR) is used as the monetary policy instrument for achieving the target inflation rate. In October 2011, core inflation hit a high of 30.8%. This resulted in severe monetary tightening by BOU, which raised the CBR to 23%, maintaining that rate for the next three months.

Commercial banks reacted by raising their lending rates[3], which affected not only the new credit but also loans taken out on a floating-rate basis prior to the CBR announcement. This caused uproar among consumers, especially the business community. Subsequently, when BOU responded to ease inflation by reducing

---

[3] Intermediation margins in Uganda have remained close to 10% for the last two decades irrespective of the BOU's policy framework.

the CBR, lending rates fell but did so more slowly and to a lesser degree than the reduction in CBR. The graph in Figure 1 shows the inflation, the CBR, and the average lending rates on shilling-denominated loans since July 2011.

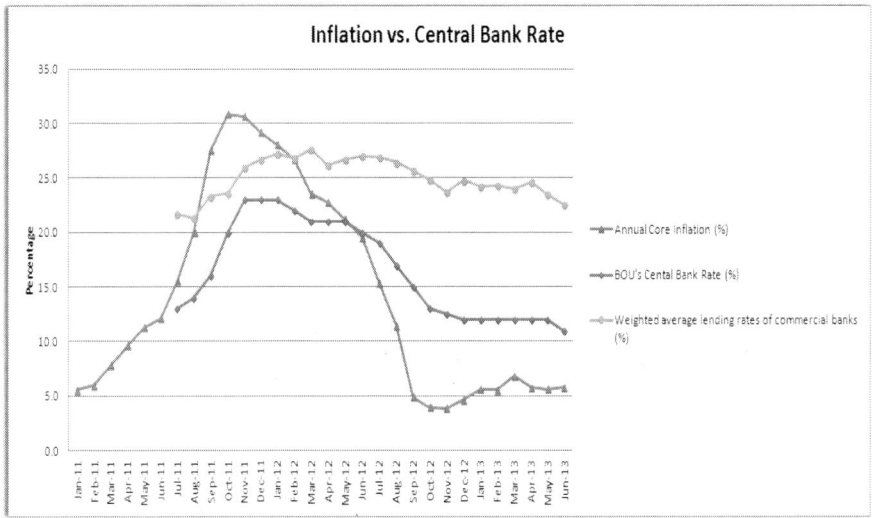

Source: Bank of Uganda website

Figure 1: Comparing Banks' Lending Rates to the Central Bank Rate

Long-term borrowing at higher interest rates required commercial banks to lend at high interest rates. As they explained, this resulted in a slow response to easing monetary policy.

There may be some truth to this. However, in a competitive credit market, banks are often unable to completely pass on increases in costs to consumers and must absorb a large proportion of any increase to stay in business. Otherwise, consumers could look for another bank that's willing to offer lower interest rates. The upward-stickiness of banks' lending rates observed recently (see Figure 1) has reiterated the presence of excessive market power (oligopolistic competition) among commercial banks in Uganda.[4] The CBR is a monetary policy tool that can only be effective if the channels transmitting the effect of the CBR to the economy such as the banking channel function smoothly.

It is crucial that the financial sector play the role of an effective conduit. Greater competition between better governed banks instead of just a larger number of banks and the resulting market efficiency are important factors in making credit affordable for its participants.[5]

Access to Finance: Even if credit became affordable, what percentage of Uganda's population would it directly reach? Or would the gains remain concentrated among large corporations?

Questions such as these have motivated several financial inclusion initiatives in Uganda, with strong involvement from the Bank of Uganda as well as other regulatory bodies. The level of financial access has improved in the last several decades—with 22% of the adult population able to access formal financial services from

---

[4] Ease of access to credit is also low in Uganda, especially in rural areas due to significant transaction costs. Therefore, money lenders with interest rates more prohibitive than those of commercial banks have survived. This aspect is covered in the next section Access to Finance.
[5] *New Vision.* August 3, 2013. "Banks Stretch Hours as Mobile Competition Bites" (http://www.newvision.co.ug/news/645715-banks-stretch-hours-as-mobile-competition-bites.html)

regulated institutions. However, this still represents less than half of the global average of 50% and falls below regional levels, too. The graph in Figure 2 shows comparative statistics for access to banking services among adults in Africa.

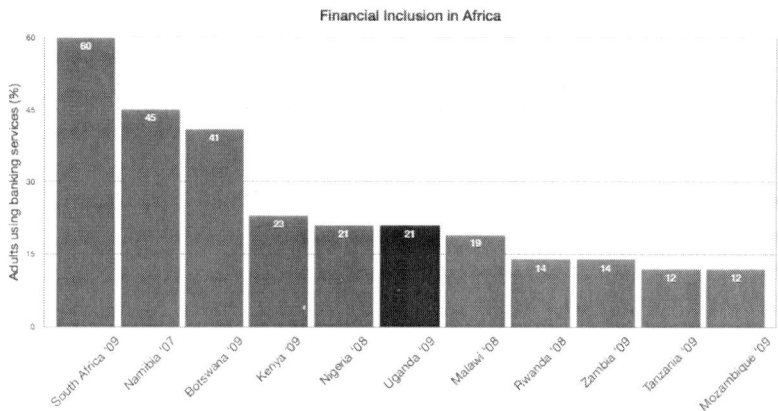

Source: Steadman/Synovate 2010

Figure 2. Financial Inclusion in Africa

The rate of financial inclusion is low due to various demand-and-supply factors. On the demand side, barriers to access include lack of understanding of financial products and services, weak property rights, and discrimination against women. On the supply side, to make the service viable for conventional commercial banks and credit institutions, the cost and difficulty of reaching the excluded population and then setting up ways to encourage repayment are prohibitive.

Several outreach and policy innovations have emerged to fill this gap. Legal reforms in the area of property rights and land titling as well as moving the National Land Registry online show promise in easing the use of property as collateral by the rightful owner. BOU and other stakeholders are driving the cause of financial literacy in financially excluded segments.

Gender-sensitive financial products are also gaining more attention because women are far less likely to be able to access finance than men in the informal financial sector in Uganda. Bringing credit institutions and micro-deposit-taking institutions under BOU's regulatory purview is a policy innovation enabling micro-financial services to appeal to a niche segment of the population. This policy will widen inclusion while ensuring the safety and reliability of these financial services.

In addition, innovations such as Mobile Money and agent banking, which work on both the supply and the demand side, are making headway. On the demand side, these methods reduce frictions such as distance and traveling costs. On the supply side, they are replacing cumbersome bank branches through the reach of mobile phones and agent networks.

Agent banking, or branchless banking, refers to the delivery of certain financial services outside conventional bank branches through third parties or agents. It expands the outreach of regulated financial services. While the number of bank branches and ATMs has increased considerably in the last few years, their locations are still concentrated in urban and suburban areas. With a well-distributed network, branchless banking will significantly boost financial access, especially in rural areas.

Financial access is often misunderstood as purely a developmental initiative to reduce poverty. But financial access not only promotes economic well-being from the grassroots; it also creates a larger market for the financial institutions in Uganda. So leaders of financial institutions would do well to recognise it is in their long-term interest to expand their reach to remote regions and untapped segments of the population.

It's time that financial access becomes recognised as a *public* good rather than an *ordinary* good. Having access to finance is an enabling factor for business success and for the economy. For instance, finance allows farmers in Gulu, a city in Northern Uganda to access small working-capital loans, which allow them to buy better quality seeds. Through a chain of value additions, this one thing can influence nutrition levels that will have significant positive spill-over effects on Ugandan society.

Availability of Information: Information goes to the heart of creating a functional and efficient market for banking services. It affects both affordability and access to finance. Asymmetry between the information available to the *providers* of financial services versus information available to the *users* hinders price discovery and reduces the number of projects that get funded.

Even if information asymmetry does not directly increase prices for financial products and services, the knowledge that consumers have limited information regarding alternative products results in market power. As they say, knowledge is power. Similarly, lending rates are often higher to account for potential risks when banks have limited means to verify the credibility of their borrowers. Therefore, eliminating information asymmetries should push the prices of financial services down.

In the presence of such information asymmetries, it's difficult for consumers to understand the risks and rewards of the products offered as well as trust the institutions and systems that hold their earnings, savings, and assets. Institutions can increase consumers' trust and access in two ways. One, they can empower the consumers themselves with financial literacy. Two, they can encourage—or mandate, if required—financial institutions to publically disclose truthful and relevant information in a form that's easy to understand.

Similarly, formal financial institutions are wary of lending to unbanked segments of the population. In the absence of hard collateral, they cannot ascertain or find credible information on the creditworthiness or income-generating capacity of people in those segments.

Another initiative to ease information asymmetries is the establishment of the credit reference bureau. Over time, access to consumers' credit history should enable banks to make informed decisions on credit requests. As a result, defaults on loans granted become less likely. In a competitive environment, lower risk on new loans should eventually drive down interest rates charged and increase the outreach of banks.

A credit reference bureau was established in Uganda in December 2008 and in the last few years, the financial identity card has been implemented. While these steps have contributed positively to improvement in financial access, there is no evidence yet of a widespread lowering of banks' interest rates.

This is not surprising. An impact on bank lending rates would be expected only when a *critical mass* of previously unbanked people are now able to access formal financial services with their new identity card. Gaps in the data collected, shortage of statistical expertise to analyse and interpret the data on credit history and other transaction costs associated with banking (e.g., ease of traveling to a nearby branch) may be some of the hindering factors.

Still, documenting consumers' credit histories so they are secure yet accessible to loan officers evaluating requests is a leap in the right direction. Information disclosure shouldn't be regarded as sunk cost to the financial service providers. In fact, as competition intensifies in the banking services market, information will become a business strategy for differentiation. Banks that are deemed safer and more reliable will develop a loyal and growing consumer base.

In a nutshell, Uganda's financial sector has developed considerably in the last five decades since independence. The challenges and disruptions it faced were debilitating, but Uganda has still emerged to become a case-study for growth in Africa. Nevertheless, the market for financial services is far from complete or perfect. Financial development as well as level of inclusion is low. In addition, oligopolistic power exists, intermediation margins are high despite BOU's drive to licence more banks,[6] and information asymmetries hamper both access and affordability. Innovative solutions that have emerged to address some of the gaps in the interaction of the demand and supply forces in Uganda should be harnessed. Financial development is possible and needed, and it should be driven by both enabling the market mechanism and, where necessary, mitigating any risks to its stability.

---

[6] Bank profitability has declined and is now comparable to other countries in East Africa, in part because of the expansion by commercial banks.

Financial Stability in Uganda: Much Ado About Nothing?

When I tell people about my work on financial stability and crisis preparedness in Uganda, they often look at me with amazement and ask, "Does Uganda need to worry about financial stability? Shouldn't financial growth or inclusion be keeping them awake at night, rather than any imminent financial crisis?" In essence, they're suggesting that the global financial crisis of 2007, which was rooted in overexposure of financial institutions to complex instruments and product structuring, is unlikely to occur in a developing country with limited capital markets to begin with.

On first glance, this sweeping logic may appear fine, even obvious. Uganda has a relatively small and developing financial sector. The ratio of private sector credit to GDP is barely 20%. Moreover, the percentage of banked population is 22% of Uganda's total adult population. Thus quite a small percentage of the total population is being exposed to the formal financial sector and its risks.

Complex derivatives and structured products such as Credit Default Swaps, Special Purpose Vehicles, Options, and so on are practically absent, with the exception of repurchase agreements and foreign exchange swaps. The insurance sector is small, and capital markets are limited in both market capitalisation of listed companies and volumes traded. Corporate bond issuances are negligible and government securities are the primary fixed-income investment instrument available. However, for a developing country, all this isn't unusual.

It may appear that debating financial stability in Uganda is premature. However, a wise man digs a well before he gets thirsty. Creating market-based regulatory and legal frameworks for financial stability in Uganda are important pre-emptive measures, even though the situation may not appear urgent.

Relevance of Financial Stability Analysis and Reform

Why waste valuable resources on financial stability regulation when financial access is at such a low level? In fact, regulatory burdens may make it more difficult and costly for commercial banks to reach out to the poorest and remotest segments, which could potentially further hamper financial inclusion. These are common arguments. And, yes, this trade-off exists, so the concern is valid.

However, resources have been dedicated to financial access and inclusion initiatives not only through the Ministry of Finance and Bank of Uganda but also through donor initiatives. Such efforts have made a difference but hindrances still persist. Thus, lack of resources could not be the prime obstacle.

In my opinion, the binding constraints to inclusion in Uganda involve an array of altogether different factors—on both supply and demand sides. On the supply side, market structure of the commercial banking industry keeps fees and lending rates high. Likewise, the cost of reaching out with full-fledged branches and ATMs in remote areas makes this commercially unviable for the banks. On the demand side, the lack of adequate or suitable collateral, weak property rights enforcement, low levels of education especially among women, and financial illiteracy are factors that hinder financial inclusion.

In fact, instead of adding to transaction costs, financial stability regulation and enforcement may *increase* financial inclusion. Owing to historical experiences, the key ingredient is bolstering public confidence in the safety and soundness of financial institutions. In the last decade, BOU closed or took over several banks to protect depositors against bad governance.

In addition, the newspapers are often rife with news of mismanagement and embezzlement in the unregulated financial firms. As a result, most people simply *do not trust* financial institutions. They'd rather stash their income under the pillow or save it with a moneylender "uncle" than deposit it into a bank—even when there's a bank branch in a town close by.

As an example, my house-helper in Uganda would rather use her cash for building a home in Gulu than save it in the financial system. She reasons that a brick-and-mortar structure provides greater tangibility, visibility, and perceived safety. Similarly, our security guard's wife "invests" in cows in her village near Mpigi rather than putting her money in banks or the local savings and credit cooperatives.

The majority of retail consumers in Uganda are financially less savvy and more inexperienced—and more wary of common financial products such as fixed deposits, loans, mortgages, and insurance—than consumers in developed countries. High interest rates also prevent retail consumers and small and medium enterprises (SMEs) from accessing credit.

In general, many consumers avoid credit because they don't trust financial institutions, find them impersonal or opaque, or have unmet or misplaced expectations. Example complaints: *I didn't know I couldn't withdraw my fixed-deposit savings for a year, and now I need money for medicine. The bank is cheating me; it didn't explain the rules right from the start.* Or: *I remember a fraud in a bank some years back. What if I lose my money?* Or: *I know of a bank that went under. Better to put my money under my mattress.*

These complaints are common in nationwide survey responses as well as in conversations at local shops.

Consumer Confidence Needed: The only way to solve this lack of trust is through creating confidence in the formal financial system, with financial literacy playing a major role. As more anecdotal evidence emerges about how local people grew their businesses with bank loans and not about foreclosures made by banks, consumer confidence will increase.

Soundness and stability are needed. Safer and more reliable financial systems will encourage access, which is already increasing through mobile phone payments and agent banking. In Uganda, the trade-off between financial stability reform and financial inclusion is not as substantial as it's often assumed to be; in fact, the two reinforce each other.

Effect of Regulation on Growth: Yet another trade off must be addressed. When private sector credit represents such a low proportion of the national gross domestic product (GDP), why worry about stability? Growth can only be good, so why sabotage it with regulatory burdens?

The post-crisis agenda of governments and central banks is revolving around better supervision of individual financial institutions as well as strengthening the financial system as a whole. Financial stability regulations, especially in the post-financial crisis era of 2007 onward, often take the form of higher capital requirements for systemically important banks (those "too important to fail"). They also include counter-cyclical capital buffers across the entire banking industry and promote restructuring of balance sheets towards more liquid assets, less leverage, and so on.

Inevitably, some of the regulatory reforms being proposed will have a dampening effect on economic growth. For example, more liquid instruments produce a more liquid balance sheet. This practice is useful during times of liquidity stress but provides a lower return during normal times. Capital that needs to be held as a buffer could have been used to lend, facilitate investments, and promote growth of the bank and the economy (assuming the investment is sound).

This issue is more pertinent for countries such as Uganda than developed countries. Developing countries have just started on a journey of unprecedented growth that promises to lift hundreds of thousands out of poverty. In that context, compromising growth will be, and should be, taken more seriously than in rich nations. Important investments in infrastructure projects, education, and health could suffer if developing economies jump on the bandwagon of macro-prudential regulation without evaluating the tools in their local context. Fortunately, Bank of Uganda evaluates, adapts, and calibrates these tools carefully to balance growth and stability in the local economic context.

Undoubtedly, growth is good and even essential, particularly for developing countries. However, the reasons for low credit-to-GDP (C/GDP) ratios include the following:

- Low financial access
- Financial institutions that have yet to reap efficiency gains from economies of scale
- Structural factors in Uganda's economy (e.g., slow growth of manufacturing because of low agricultural productivity, which ties down labour in the sector)

Impact studies are needed to determine exactly the degree to which each of these factors has a dampening effect. However, financial stability can bring reliability to credit offered by financial institutions, leading to better uptake and higher C/GDP in Uganda. Here, too, I believe stability can help growth rather than dampen it.

The pace of growth matters equally. An unsustainably high growth rate of credit could signal risk. At some point, the industry would realize that the rapid pace of growth isn't supported by commensurate growth in economic activity.

As household indebtedness and corporate leverage increase, the financial system becomes more vulnerable to a sudden reversal in the cycle. Therefore, not only is financial stability relevant to developing countries because of the systemic risk that could emerge, but it also contributes to financial development.

Important questions to ask include:

- Are the dampening effects short term or long term?
- Do they hurt current output or impair the economy's capacity to produce?
- In the absence of such measures, what is the expected level of output loss if a systemic crisis were to occur? (*Note:* They occur more often in middle-income countries than in rich countries.[7])

Systemic Risks: Many tools proposed by the global caucus of financial stability experts are aimed at mitigating common risks in developed financial systems. The post-crisis regulatory agenda is evidently skewed towards solving problems in *advanced* financial systems. Few analyses are being conducted of whether these measures are relevant and effective in *developing* financial systems. It's almost as if the international best practices implicitly assume that financial stability concerns are similar in small, developing economies as in those with advanced economies. This assumption implies that any solutions to such concerns would be a subset of (or simplified versions of) those implemented in advanced economies, rather than being fundamentally different and customised to the local context.

---

[7] IMF Working Paper 2015. "Credit Booms and Macroeconomic Dynamics: Stylized Facts and Lessons for Low-Income Countries." Marco Arena, Serpil Bouza, Era Dabla-Norris, Kerstin Gerling, Lamin Njie.

(https://www.imf.org/external/pubs/ft/wp/2015/wp1511.pdf)

I would argue the opposite. Financial stability and risks to it can in fact, be more pronounced and debilitating in developing countries than in advanced ones. However, the forms that financial stability regulations or reforms may take depend on the types of risks predominant in a given context. Where complex financial centres may be developing tools to mitigate speculation or market risks, the nature of risks in Uganda is different. Mitigating credit risk or liquidity concerns may be more relevant there. In other words, the nature and focus of financial stability surveillance and analysis differs from economy to economy.

Let's not forget that common factors exist, too. For instance, financial cycles result in upturns/downturns in prices and employment levels in both developed and developing countries. Because of this, both advanced and developing economies need countercyclical measures. A rapid growth in the price of assets such as real estate could well lead to asset price bubbles in low-income countries, just as they could in developed markets. The risks to the financial system from credit cycles and their amplifying effect on asset prices is well documented. I would argue that "pro-cyclicality" is more pronounced in developing countries such as Uganda, Rwanda, Burundi, and others that have underdeveloped or small capital markets than they are in developed countries. As a result, these countries experience a lack of viable investment alternatives to private-sector lending during periods of economic booms or expansionary monetary policy.

Some types of behavioural phenomena such as herding and panic led to bank runs and insolvencies of banks during the 2007-2009 global financial crisis (e.g., Northern Rock, U.K.). Such contagion can occur even in less sophisticated financial markets and banking sectors than the U.K.

In fact, in developing financial systems where information asymmetries among the investors, creditors, and borrowers are considerable, such events are more likely to happen than in well-established economies. Therefore, financial stability is a focal point for prudential authorities in advanced and developing economies alike, even though the nature and focus of the regulations and reforms differ.

A Developing Country's Approach to Financial Stability

Financial systems can learn important practices from the international dialogue on financial stability. The arsenal that prudential authorities develop for themselves in economies such as Uganda would be a mix of home-grown solutions and international best practices adapted to the local context. They would need to strike a fine balance between innovation and stability of financial services, institutions, and systems. While there's a need to optimise growth, experiencing a recklessly maximised growth would be more harmful than beneficial in the long run.

To analyse financial stability, a qualitative understanding of the economy—all aspects of it including labour market dynamics—is necessary. It is ideal to have in place a composite indicator or set of indicators for systemic risk. Such measures should take into account the various types of risks, such as market risk, credit risk, liquidity risk, interest rate risk, contagion risk, and even sovereign risk.

However, challenges are associated with developing and using such a composite indicator. First, developing and fine-tuning a composite indicator is a data-intensive process, so having reliable and preferably high-frequency data on risk measures is important. Many developing countries don't have this data readily available or have only begun to collect it.

Second, if such an indicator is developed, interpreting its results in a useful way for macro-prudential policy-making is more an art than a science. The role of expert judgement can't be over-emphasised. Therefore, many central bankers believe a composite measure that provides a single rating for risk may be losing too much in aggregation. Instead, it's better to have a set, or dashboard, of multiple indicators that, together, paint a picture of the level of financial stability in the system.

At the Bank of Uganda, I had the opportunity to do work on evaluating the effectiveness of indicators to be used in Uganda for calibrating Basel III countercyclical capital buffer[8]. I realised that while credit-to-GDP ratio was a reliable leading indicator for systemic risk in most western European economies, in Uganda's context (similar to many other developing countries) it often produced false signals.

Lack of historical time series data for the financial sector before the 1990s and the relatively recent creation of capital markets in Uganda make it nearly impossible to construct and evaluate many other such indicators. However, Bank of Uganda along with the Statistics Bureau is actively pioneering the creation of a real estate pricing index which may allow them to evaluate house prices as leading indicators of credit market stress in Uganda. Inevitably for Uganda, simple analytical methods and a healthy amount of judgement formed through seasoned experience of the ups and downs of the credit cycle is indispensable alongside the use of quantitative measures such as credit-to-GDP ratio or real estate prices.

Having these factors in place would facilitate policy-making towards the twin goals of growth and stability. The prudential

---

[8] Bank of Uganda Working Paper Series - WP No. 11/2013. "Credit-to-GDP as a forward-looking indicator of systemic credit risk - A critical evaluation using data from Uganda" Prajakta Kharkar Nigam

(http://www.bou.or.ug/export/sites/default/bou/bou-downloads/research/BouWorkingPapers/2013/All/WP-11-2013---Credit-to-GDP-as-a-forward-looking-Indicator-of-Systemic-Credit-Risk--A-Critical-Evaluation-using-data-from-Uganda.pdf) regulatory authorities and central banks should be enablers for market-led growth. Having adequate data, analytical tools, and metrics suitable for the local context would allow developing countries to embrace such growth while minimising financial imbalances.

Innovation in Payment Systems

Safe and efficient payment systems catalyse financial inclusion and economic growth. In East Africa, payments enabled through mobile phone networks have been a key innovation in retail payments. Naturally, regulatory authorities in Uganda have been keenly observing their growth and performance. This essay attempts to understand why some innovations in retail payments such as mobile money become widespread while others wither.

Drivers of Innovation in the Payments Market

Innovation in retail payment occurs from two standpoints: payment platforms and products offered through those platforms. Bank branches, ATMs, point of sale (POS) terminals, and the Internet exemplify innovative platforms, whereas credit/debit card, e-money, and mobile money are innovative payment products. The electronic modes of payment and e-money together allow online remittances—a payment innovation.

Innovation in payment systems often begins as a supply-side phenomenon. Nevertheless, for its uptake and growth, a particular mix of demand-and-supply-side conditions is needed in the market. Unmet demand from a segment, potentially high profit margins, and low barriers to entry (usually a liberal regulatory environment) attract new payment service providers into the market. These new entrants either provide payment services in a more appealing way than the incumbents or innovate at a more fundamental level by introducing new platforms or products.

In the former case, increasing competition encourages the incumbents to invest in innovations. In the latter, the incumbent firms jump on the bandwagon to provide the new service through partnerships, superior distribution networks, or predatory pricing against the entering firms. In essence, incumbents adjust their business models to preserve their market share. This competitive pressure generates a feedback loop, which gets the entire industry thinking about how to innovate further and faster to stay ahead of the competition. As a result, consumers benefit with lower transaction costs, lower prices, and better quality services.

The trajectory of innovation in payment systems is similar to that of any other industry. However, during my time in Kampala, it intrigued me that some innovations in payments showed rapid uptake while others lagged. Why the difference?

Once an innovative product has established itself with a critical mass of consumers, its growth depends on demand-side factors. These include eliminating transaction costs, reducing charges for consumers, and *reliability*—perhaps the most important factor in the weakly institutionalised markets of Uganda.

Prior to introduction, the market is concentrated and oligopolistic at best. Profitability is substantial. As a result, consumers are often paying exorbitant charges for payment services in the market and have few alternatives for switching. Yet, high price doesn't guarantee quality. The payment services offered usually cater to the needs of a limited segment. Some segments in Uganda, such as the informally banked and the financially excluded, are completely neglected by conventional payment services. This occurs due to a number of frictions or transaction costs.

In a market that's imperfectly competitive, payment providers are able to completely pass on to the consumer the technological and operational costs of providing the service. As a result, the charges become prohibitively high. Innovations that create price-based competition in the market often lead to lowering of such charges for customers and thus see a greater uptake.

However, other transaction costs may still persist. Requirements for signing up for some payment services can include the time, money, and travel distance needed to obtain information or accumulate documents, for example.

Moreover, in the absence of a clear regulatory guideline, uncertainty regarding the reliability of firms that provide payment services remains a key friction that could prevent people from trusting and signing up for a new offering. Experience in various countries suggests innovations that gain efficiency by eliminating such frictions actually bring down transaction costs and enjoy greater adoption rates.

Mobile Payments—Poster Child for Innovation in East Africa

Mobile money transfer services have been in operation in Uganda since March 2009. In 2012, Warid Telecom became the fourth mobile money service provider through its networks by introducing Warid Pesa. The other three include MTN Mobile Money, UTL's M-Sente, and Airtel's Zap.

At the 2013 Evidence on Innovations in Savings and Payments Policy Conference in Kampala, Bank of Uganda's Director of Financial Stability Dr. Charles Abuka gave the keynote address. He said there had been a steep rise in both the number and value of mobile payments in Uganda between 2009 and 2013. Lately, however, mobile money growth has been stabilising. This may be attributed to increasing competition by retail payment providers as well as adjustment in marketing tactics by banks providing payment services.

Today, the supply-and-demand-side factors in Uganda have come together to create a fertile ground for innovations such as mobile money, agent banking, and plastic card payments.

On the supply side, profitability has been high among banks, which were the main providers of payment services prior to mobile money. Bank of Uganda has been liberal in allowing innovations. At the same time, it monitors them to determine whether the new payment system has become systemically important and warrants oversight, guidelines, or even licensing and regulation. Therefore, barriers to entry for new payment system providers have been relatively moderate.

A large segment of financially excluded adults whose needs are as yet unmet represents a potentially profitable untapped market. As such, it's drawing interest from telecommunication firms entering the retail payments market in Uganda. On the demand side, in Uganda as well as the East Africa region, the reach of banking services, and thus financial inclusion, is low.

(See Figure 3.)

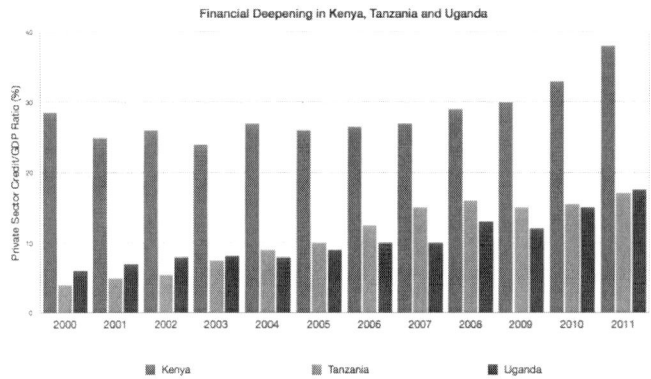

Source: World Bank Databank

Figure 3: Financial Deepening in Kenya, Tanzania and Uganda

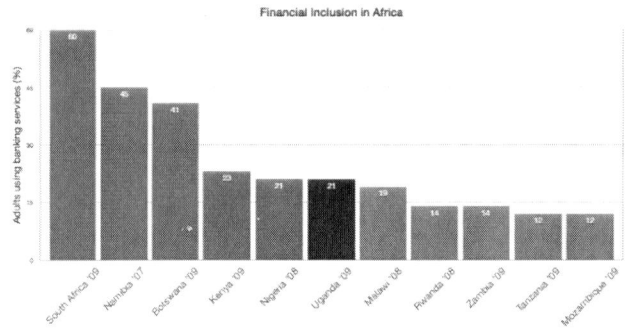

Source: Steadman/Synovate 2010

Figure 4: Financial Inclusion in Africa

Not all banks have branches or ATMs in the remote areas of the country, so bank-led payment services are impractical for many rural consumers. However, mobile phone penetration is high, even in rural areas.

The penetration of formal financial institutions is severely limited compared to that of mobile money agents and mobile phone network coverage in Uganda. As of 2013, in the Kampala region alone, the number of mobile money agents is nearly eight-fold that of bank branches, microfinance institutions (MFIs) and savings and credit cooperative organisations (SACCOs). In rural areas, the gap is even more gaping. For example, as of 2013, in the Mbarara region in south-west Uganda, the reach of mobile money agents is close to 20 times that of formal and semi-formal financial institutions[9].

Similarly, charges on mobile phone payments are relatively low compared to those on Real Time Gross Settlement (RTGS) remittances through banks. As a result, making payments from mobile phones has quickly slashed the transaction costs for the consumer in terms of money, distance, and time.

In addition, mobile money in Uganda has provided a viable alternative to other payment services, and for some segments of the population, it was the only channel for participating in the payments market without the risks associated with handling cash.

---

[9] Bill and Melinda Gates Foundation, Financial Services for the Poor (FSP) Interactive Maps (www.fspmaps.com)

Will Mobile Money Be the New Face of Payments Everywhere?

While we may understand which factors facilitated the exponential growth of mobile money in Uganda, I don't think we can be sure that it will meet the same fate everywhere. The same innovation may have a vastly different performance in different markets, depending on the local context. Mobile money fulfilled an unmet need for the large majority of people without access to a bank account and for banked consumers who found the remittance charges prohibitive in Uganda and Kenya.

On the other hand, in South Africa where the number of people who don't have a bank account is small, mobile money hasn't grown as rapidly. Instead, the country has introduced the WIZZIT mobile banking solution, which connects existing banking infrastructure with the mobile network. In Uganda and Kenya, Mobile Money and M-Pesa mobile remittance services have enabled person-to-person and person-to-business transfers, cash deposits, and withdrawals at designated outlets. They also handle loan receipts or repayments without any need for a bank account. By comparison, in the Philippines, a combination of bank-led and non-bank-led payment innovations took flight through the bank-led model Mobile Money SMART and the Mobile Network Operator or MNO-led model GLOBE CASH.

In Brazil, a "correspondent banking" model arose with over 95,000 business establishments, including post offices. It became the most popular channel for credit transfers and bill payments, and government agencies use it to pay social benefits using the popular point of sale (POS) device and card.

Similarly, in China, multipurpose prepaid cards issued by non-banks and used at POS terminals by unbanked persons have shown promising growth. Mexico as well has introduced tiered deposit accounts and prepaid cards for the purpose of social benefit transfers.

While competition is increasing in the retail payment industry in Uganda, the mobile money market in particular is still far from saturated. Market shares are concentrated, and the large telecom providers such as MTN have market power. With competition from agent banking as well as other providers of retail payment services such as Safaricom, hopefully market power will decline, mobile money agents will become empowered, and a decline in charges will happen.

An overarching framework for oversight of payment innovations has become a core responsibility of central banks. The banks monitor existing and planned systems, assessing them against the objectives of safety and efficiency and, where necessary, they induce change.

Mobile money has been growing so rapidly that it may become a systemically important payment system in Uganda. Therefore, the need would arise to limit possible systemic risks. The Central Bank and other high-level bodies responsible for macro-prudential policy and financial stability would be wise to continue to vigilantly monitor such innovations in retail payment. In fact, any oversight may contribute to the soundness and reliability of mobile money contributing to adoption rates.

Towards the end of my fellowship, I had an opportunity to contribute to discussions around drafting a payments system oversight policy for Uganda. While the topic of oversight calls for an article on its own, I would like to note several pertinent issues needing to be addressed in determining an optimal oversight framework for payment systems, especially innovations.

As digital payments become less and less intermediated, there are concerns about enforcing adequate KYC requirements, regulating cross border mobile payments and mitigation of money laundering. There are also privacy and security concerns related to mobile payments data. Should mobile network operators, credit reference bureaus, or regulatory authorities be hosting the data on payment transactions? To what extent should this information influence the credit scores of consumers? I suggest the challenge for regulatory authorities be to ensure a level playing field for all entities offering similar payment services.

Eventually, the nature of oversight will be a key factor in determining how the landscape for payment innovation evolves. And for a change, the rest of the world is looking to learn from African countries' experience as pioneers in the area of mobile payment innovations.

Chinese Development Aid to Uganda

"I'll make you an offer you can't refuse." This famous line from Mario Puzo's classic *The Godfather* comes to mind when I think about China's development efforts in Uganda. In Alon Mwesigwa's article (July 23, 2013) in *The Observer* titled "Tracking Chinese Money in Uganda,"[10] he asks two pertinent questions:

1. Is the quality of Chinese projects good enough?
2. Is Uganda fully aware of and factoring in the true cost of such development assistance from China?

Essentially, he's suggesting that the "offer" may not be as tempting as it seems.

Ideally, any country would pursue development through its own resources, for there's dignity in self-reliance. Resources can consist of either fiscal revenues or financing from domestic capital markets. Where neither is feasible, however, countries look for financing from other countries or international organisations.

---

[10] *The Observer*, "Tracking Chinese Money in Uganda." Alon Mwesigwa, July 23, 2013. (http://www.observer.ug/index.php?option=com_content&view=article&id=26562:tracking-chinese-money-in-uganda&catid=38:business&Itemid=68)

In Uganda-China partnerships, most of the critical Chinese projects in Uganda are funded through non-concessional loans—for example, the Karuma dam and the Isimba power project. Yet, for those which are not, it is important to clearly understand whether China's development efforts are grants (a free lunch) or a disguised loan with implicit deferred repayment. (The latter would, of course, be a free lunch for Uganda today but at the expense of its future income.) My hunch is that China provides help against an implicit expectation of preferential treatment or "returns" from Uganda's growing natural resources sector in the future. If this is true, then China's "aid" is more like a foreign policy of investment than an altruistic grant. To decide on any loan, Uganda needs to 1) evaluate the offer on its own merits and demerits using a cost-benefit analysis, and 2) evaluate the offer compared to the country's next best alternative. Doing a cost-benefit analysis is essential.

Cost-Benefit Analysis

The benefit side in a cost-benefit analysis involves:

- infrastructure development that Uganda may not be able to accomplish with its own strained resources,
- timely completion, and
- potentially an accelerated move out of poverty for thousands.

In addition to the direct impact through widening fiscal and current account deficits on Ugandan shilling's depreciation, the cost side also includes long-term implications such as:

- expectations the current Uganda government may be for future generations and governments, and
- economic cost of future repayment, which may turn out to be exorbitant in hindsight.

Assessing the costs critically: I'll evaluate only the cost side because the benefit side is self-evident. First, how much money is really at stake? Uganda needs to be realistic in pricing the expected value of its natural resources. This value is based not only on their intrinsic value and market price but also on how easy it is to benefit from that value.

For instance, the expected value of petroleum to Uganda is not merely the projected oil price times the number of barrels that can be produced. This figure should be discounted by the higher risk factors in Uganda including its weak institutions, multiple market frictions, and the fact it has no deep-sea port to export the oil. So the *true expected* value of Uganda's natural resources may be lower than touted. From a cost perspective, this means that less may be at stake than the public thinks. At the same time, it may also mean that if contracts are not optimally designed, the Ugandan economy may end up with even fewer gains than those calculated by the government when awarding contracts to Chinese companies.

Next, even if a priceless national treasure is at stake, how likely is the threat to it? To be reasonable, a doomsday scenario is not as likely as it may seem. China's foreign policy, including its development efforts in Africa, is focused on establishing China as a geopolitical power. Resource-rich Africa is its golden chip against other contenders for global power.

I find it difficult to believe that China's primary motivation is to plunder African resources or people—although either could easily happen as an unintended side-effect of capital investments. To avoid such a situation, Uganda should design mining and exploration contracts to balance incentives for firms to invest while helping the nation retain a majority of gains from national treasures. It's up to Uganda's government and an active civil society to decide whether Uganda follows in the footsteps of Botswana, which utilised its natural resources (diamonds) for propelling the country toward growth, or in those of Angola, where gains from its endowment (petroleum) have been expropriated by the powerful few and human development in the country has, in fact, deteriorated.

In addition to economic costs, Chinese contributions incur political costs. When a person or country takes aid from another, even when the donor expects no repayment, the receiver increasingly comes under a psychological indebtedness.

Well-known Stanford professor Robert Cialdini calls this the principle of reciprocity. The "soft" power the donor gains over the receiver, often inadvertently, builds covertly. As this happens, the receiver subconsciously looks for ways to repay the donor and often does so by acquiescing to or even appeasing the donor.

While a kind or benevolent donor would not misuse such power, a less than benevolent one could use it to elicit further benefits from the receiver. So therefore the question to carefully think about is this: *Is China a benevolent donor?*

The jury is still out on whether intangible costs are outweighed by the benefits to Uganda from Chinese development assistance. Large projects are indeed built in a timely manner by Chinese firms; however, as Alon Mwesigwa pointed out, the quality may be uncertain. Yet, the benefits appear to be significant. China may export inferior quality electronics, but the country has been rapidly building a high-speed rail network that will become the most extensive in the world when completed. In cities such as Shanghai and Guangzhou, skyscrapers emerge at remarkable speeds.

So, in general, there's reason to believe Chinese firms have gained expertise in building sound infrastructure over the years. Also, the onus for ensuring quality should be on Uganda as the recipient. Therefore, Uganda's government should insist on carrying out due diligence on contracted firms by checking records and disallowing any black-listed firms from bidding.

Next Best Alternative: Technocrats in Uganda should undertake due diligence and analyse proposed projects to determine their suitability, their sequencing, and their impact on the country's macroeconomic framework. In doing so, it is essential to carefully evaluate their options comparatively rather than each on its own merits and demerits as long as they meet certain minimum criteria for safety and durability.

Thus, instead of considering whether the quality of Chinese construction, exploration, or medical equipment is good, they should ask if the quality is better than Uganda's next best alternative. And what, then, is Uganda's next best alternative? Does this alternative outweigh the costs and exceed the benefits of the Chinese efforts?

Then the experts consider which course of action 1) helps improve skills of the local labour force, 2) brings growth commensurate with the increase in debt burden, if any, 3) has the potential to self-finance itself (e.g., through road tolls), and 4) brings the country closer to self-reliance.

With these considerations in mind, the willingness of the Chinese to donate medical equipment and award scholarships to Ugandan students can be applauded. These items clearly enhance Uganda's human capital.

However, the Chinese firms in Uganda often import Chinese labour on a large scale. In that case, do the skills transfer to the local workers? Of course, the Chinese could lament the level of productivity and motivation of the local labour force; however, that's a separate debate. If the skills of local labour are not being enhanced, capacity-building for Uganda's local labour force may be at risk with an over-involvement of Chinese labour.

A steady supply of loans and the import of skilled labour from China may seem like a convenient option. Yet, bear in mind that such "generosity" can lead to indebtedness and technical dependence that could cost Uganda more than expected.

Note: This article was originally published online on the blog Africa at LSE.

Tax Avoidance in Uganda

In the quest for financial self-reliance, taxation is a key source of income for most governments. In turn, citizens expect government officials to spend tax revenue on public services.

Failure to file and pay taxes is illegal *tax evasion*. However, people work around the law and find loopholes to avoid paying at least some of their taxes. This is called *tax avoidance*.

In theory, a government can orchestrate a crackdown on tax *evasion* and take action against those found guilty. On the other hand, the state has no legal recourse against those who practice tax *avoidance*, because these people haven't done anything illegal. Uganda presents an intriguing case study for tax avoidance. Experts agree that Uganda's tax system conforms to global benchmarks, with Uganda's income and corporate tax rates being 40% per annum at the highest bracket.[11] However, in the period from 2005 to 2015, tax revenues contributed only 11.7% to the country's GDP.[12] This leaves a large, worrisome gap between the amount of tax

---

[11] *The Observer*. July 24, 2012. "URA explains how to calculate your PAYE" by Robert Wamala Lumanyika. (http://observer.ug/business/38-business/20011-ura-explains-how-to-calculate-your-paye-)

[12] *New Vision*, February 12, 2015. "Increase Agriculture Revenue to Boost Tax Contribution to GDP" (http://www.newvision.co.ug/news/664782-increase-agriculture-revenue-to-boost-tax-contribution-to-gdp.html)

expected and the tax actually paid on the overall earnings of its citizens.[13]

A number of technical factors contribute to this gap, including inaccurate capture of the service sector by GDP calculations. However, the disparate numbers also highlight the extent of tax evasion and tax avoidance in the country.

Tax avoidance is not always intentional. It occurs due to the existence of a large informal sector not captured by the tax regime, as well as ignorance among the masses about tax matters.

The Ugandan government can do three things to reduce the current amount of tax avoidance: 1) improve the legal framework to weed out opportunities for tax avoidance, 2) create better incentives for tax payment, and 3) promote far-reaching awareness regarding tax matters that persuades people to pay their taxes. Let's review each of these.

Improve the Legal Framework: How is it that the contribution of revenue from the construction sector to GDP is 8%, but the contribution of this sector to taxes is a mere 2%?[14] Likewise, real estate activities contribute 4% to GDP but only 1% to tax revenues.

---

[13] Whether the taxation rate should be high or low and which form taxes should take (income, VAT, investment taxes) are important issues, but that's for a different debate.

[14] *New Vision*, February 12, 2015. "Increase Agriculture Revenue to Boost Tax Contribution to GDP" (http://www.newvision.co.ug/news/664782-increase-agriculture-revenue-to-boost-tax-contribution-to-gdp.html)

Tightening the legal framework and thus closing loopholes is imperative to slowly weed out possibilities of tax avoidance. A step towards the right direction for tax proposals in the 2015/2016 budget include the requirement to have registered Tax Identification Numbers. This would be necessary for any individual to be able to conduct business activity and apply for permits of any sort. [15] However, how effective these will be depends on how strictly they are enforced. A clever way to do so would be to employ the tax lawyers and consultants who make a living helping firms and individuals "creatively" *minimize* their legal tax burden. However, the government would have to remunerate them generously to entice them to come over to "the other side."

Moreover, "political will" plays a potent role. For instance, President Museveni's backing for and public sensitization on the need for a Value-added Tax (VAT) enabled its introduction in the 1990s, despite protests from the business community who feared its dampening effect on economic activity.

Create Better Incentives for Tax Payment: A more creative and constructive approach would be increasing incentives for people to pay their taxes. For example, the tax system could be reorganised to offer tax rebates on investments that help finance

---

[15] Article by Sheilla Atim, a lawyer and popular blogger in Uganda (http://sheillokeny.blogspot.ca/2015/09/new-tax-laws-in-uganda-20142015.html)

the government's developmental work. Perhaps discounts could be offered on government loans to university students whose parents are able to show three years of filing tax returns.

A key reason people don't pay taxes is they don't see their tax money improving the public services that directly affect their lives. For example, the urban populace doesn't relate to better roads in rural areas, and the rich don't use public infrastructure such as public schools and public transportation as much as the poor do. Like it or not, the altruistic incentive for paying taxes so other citizens can benefit is limited.

One approach to solving the problem is creating new public services and improving existing ones for all the people who should pay taxes. Such improvements need to be explicitly communicated to the public through various channels.

In addition, even well-meaning citizens are discouraged from paying their taxes by government corruption. The public perceives corruption as a leakage of tax revenue into a bottomless pit, thus it seems unfair for taxpayers to keep paying into the system. According to the 2012 East African Bribery Survey,[16] Uganda has topped the list of countries most prone to corruption in the region.

---

[16] *The East African.* September 1, 2012. "Uganda most corrupt in EA- report" Gaaki Kigambo.
(http://www.theeastafrican.co.ke/business/Uganda+most+corrupt+in+EA++report+/-/2560/1492468/-/bx1493z/-/index.html)

Indeed, the Ugandan police force and judiciary have been identified as the most bribery-prone institutions across East Africa.

The government could rebuild the public's confidence through proactive measures such as using taxes to improve police salaries and put in place systems for accountability. These would produce a marked decline in future police corruption. If hapless drivers who haven't even committed traffic offenses are no longer stopped for bribes, people will certainly notice.

While small changes in petty corruption aren't adequate to stop tax avoidance altogether, they can help make citizens more civic-conscious and therefore more inclined to pay taxes. Without a doubt, however, Uganda can't expect a significant reversal in tax avoidance unless people see an obvious decline in public-office corruption.

Promote Far-Reaching Awareness Regarding Tax Matters: Widening the tax base is key to bridging the gap between the *expected* tax revenue and the tax amounts actually *collected*. The existence of a large informal economy contributes to this gap. To close that gap, the government can expand the tax base to include informal sectors (e.g., agricultural services and household labour) and then improve tax compliance of this wider base.

Currently, the agricultural sector contributes 27% to the GDP of Uganda but only 0.8% to the tax revenues.[17]

A large percentage of the citizenry lacks awareness about the potential benefits of paying taxes. The government can reach out to this untapped tax base through persuasive education on tax matters.

Key Influencers: In an interview published in the *Daily Monitor* in June 2012,[18] Francis Kamulegeya, senior partner at PricewaterhouseCoopers (PwC), Uganda, noted that key influencers in the society can play a pivotal role. He made the case that cultural and religious leaders would be more effective than politicians and civil servants in persuading the public that paying taxes matters for the country's progress as well as for future generations.

Mr. Kamulegeya pointed out that churches in Uganda receive religious donations amounting to 10% of every devotee's income without any need for reminders. People readily give to the church because they perceive it directly benefits them, their families, and their religious communities. One strategy, then, would be for the government to appeal to local pastors to educate churchgoers on

---

[17] *New Vision*, February 12, 2015. "Increase Agriculture Revenue to Boost Tax Contribution to GDP" (http://www.newvision.co.ug/news/664782-increase-agriculture-revenue-to-boost-tax-contribution-to-gdp.html)

[18] *Daily Monitor*. June 12, 2012. "Experts Speak Out on the State of Uganda's Economy" Nicholas Kalungi (http://www.monitor.co.ug/Business/Prosper/Experts+speak+out+on+the+state+of+Uganda+s+economy/-/688616/1425016/-/2lubf7z/-/index.html)

how paying taxes has, for example, funded a new road or dispensary in the town. It's likely the churchgoing community would trust pastors over government officials and thus respond better to a message about paying taxes.

In conclusion, developing countries may face similar tax issues as those in the developed world, but because the underlying reasons are different, so are the solutions. Tax evasion is a serious issue that can't be ignored. In Uganda's case, equally important is the task of reducing tax avoidance among well-meaning citizens. Those include people who are disillusioned, distrusting, disengaged from the formal economy, or simply misinformed about potential long-term benefits of paying taxes. These problems may seem easier to tackle than tax evasion. However, doing so will require a better understanding of the local context and more creativity than the hard hand of the law.

Note: A previous version of this article was originally published online on the blog Africa at LSE on 24 September 2012.

Regulation Not a Panacea for SACCO Troubles

In the last century, we have witnessed rapid technological innovation. At one time, the list of basic human needs began with food, clothing, shelter, and ended with education, health, and sanitation.

However, in the information age, two new items have been added to the list: the Internet and financial access. The mobile phone revolution in East Africa brought Internet access to the masses, but unfortunately, financial access is still far from ubiquitous. Formal financial services reach less than one-fifth of the population in Uganda, and informal sector financial services only increase this to around half the population at best. In other words, half the country is unable to reap the savings in good times and borrowing in times of need. In fact, those who have access through informal institutions and arrangements are likely being exploited, cheated, or offered grossly inefficient services.

SACCOs in Uganda (like ROSCAs in Latin American countries) are savings and credit cooperatives that have emerged to fill this gap. Cooperative savings arrangements and microfinance initiatives have achieved significant success and generally a clean reputation in otherwise corruption-ridden countries such as Bangladesh and Indonesia. I questioned why this was not the case in Uganda after reading Nathan Were's commentary in the *Daily Monitor* on October 2, 2012. His article was titled "Rural finances: Raising questions about the state of Uganda's rural financial system."[19] Were's article addresses the dismal state of governance in Uganda's savings cooperatives. Including these organisations in the regulatory ambit of financial regulatory authorities in Uganda would be the solution, he concluded.

I beg to differ. To answer the question why SACCOs in Uganda are in a state of disarray, let's go back to the features of credit cooperatives, which make them successful in other countries.

First of all, any SACCO or collective saving and lending arrangement is only as strong as its relationships with members. The basis of collective savings programs is to leverage "social capital" for ensuring that members keep their commitments and behave ethically. (Social capital means the influence that people in a community have over each other's behaviour due to their social relationships.)

---

[19] *Daily Monitor*. October 2, 2012. "Raising Questions about the state of Uganda's rural financial system" Nathan Were.
(http://www.monitor.co.ug/Business/Prosper/Raising+questions+about+the+state+of+Uganda+s+rural/-/688616/1522316/-/lomc7b/-/index.html)

Savers and borrowers prefer to keep their commitments because they value their reputation among this particular group. They behave ethically because their relationship with the community or their reputation is *too valuable to lose,* even for money!

Conversely, if they don't adhere to their commitments, other members in the group will generally be able to talk them into doing so. Therefore, at a minimum, members need to play a crucial role in the governance of the SACCO by effectively exercising this social capital.

What, then, leads to the creation and maintenance of strong social ties among group members? To ensure that social capital works, the formation, size, and composition of the member group are all critical.

Ideally, groups should be *self-selected.* In that case, all participants would be selected unanimously and share common underlying ties, such as being from the same village or working at the same place, etc. This way, any prospective members who have a history of default in that community or are considered untrustworthy get weeded out before they even join. This makes the group more close-knit and possibly more reliable to begin with. While group selection for most SACCOs in Uganda is based on such a common bond, that criterion isn't always painstakingly enforced, and exceptions are common.

Second, collective savings programs generally work well in small groups of women. A small group size makes governance less cumbersome, makes behaviour (or misbehaviour) of members more visible to other members, and therefore creates greater accountability.

For example, if a member who generally commands more influence within the group is misusing this influence to embezzle funds, this person's actions become evident easily and early. The other members discuss such transgressions in person, often during their meetings. The threat of public shaming acts as an effective deterrent for such embezzlement in small, close-knit groups. In large groups, such behaviour becomes known only when it's too late, and the relationships between members are too loose to be valuable anyway.

Today, many SACCOs are missing out on this self-governing mechanism because they're required by law to have a minimum of 30 members.[20] That number, in my opinion, is too large to form any meaningful social capital within the group, and I think the basis for this law needs a second look.

The commentary in the *Daily Monitor* suggested that lack of regulation is the cause of improper governance. However, if a SACCO is ill-governed, it points to a breakdown of the social capital within the group, which is unlikely to be rectified through external

---

[20] Uganda Cooperative Savings and Credit Union Ltd. website (http://www.ucscu.co.ug/)

regulation. Regulating inefficient financial institutions doesn't make them efficient if they're inherently designed for failure (e.g., large groups in which members don't trust or know each other well). Rather, it creates a false picture that the regulatory authorities are endorsing the business that these institutions are engaging in and the way they conduct it.

I recognise that given the structure and sizes of Ugandan SACCOs, there is a place for regulation. Regulatory guidelines can be a great resource for SACCOs to implement best practices and good accounting standards as well as be protected by some form of insolvency framework. However, I am sceptical about the assertion that regulation of SACCOs by the appropriate government authorities would solve the problem of mismanagement altogether. While there may be benefits to regulation of SACCOs, regulation itself is certainly not adequate.

First, just as markets fail, regulations can fail as well. This was amply highlighted by the microfinance crisis in the central-bank-regulated microfinance sector in Andhra Pradesh, India. The state passed new, inadequately thought-through regulation for microfinance institutions. In the aftermath, microfinance institutions in Andhra began to face large-scale defaults, which eventually led to the bankruptcy of the largest microfinance institution in the country. Clearly, regulation is not enough and, in fact, improperly implemented regulation may do more harm than good.

In my opinion, the "government-should-do-something" rhetoric no longer works. Regulating every single financial institution of every size and volume isn't practical as the economy incurs significant costs for such regulation. Instead of regulating institutions that are too large to be efficient, regulators can weed them out by letting them dissolve.

An interesting characteristic of SACCOs in Uganda is that many of them have been created as development institutions, as conduits to channel financial support from the state to the grassroots level. As such, their failure could adversely affect the reach and effectiveness of state-led development programs. An alternative approach then could be to encourage these groups to downsize to the optimal size at which micro-savings and micro-lending can effectively self-regulate. Yet another option is to encourage these groups to transform themselves into credit institutions, which are already regulated under the current framework.

It is important to acknowledge that failure of even small SACCOs could undermine the confidence in the cooperative savings system in Uganda. This is where the heavily promoted financial literacy efforts in Uganda will bear fruit.

People need to heighten their financial awareness, exercise caution, and ask sound questions when they join SACCOs. Why would they want to hand over their savings to a group that's too large for them to know and trust each member well? Yes, SACCO members often have no alternatives, but they're still advised to avoid group-based financing services they don't fully understand. When such questioning begins to happen on a large scale at the grassroots level, SACCOs will be forced to pay heed and self-regulate the size and formation of their groups.

Financial literacy initiatives implemented by BOU can go a long way to encourage people to ask these questions and make informed financial decisions. Moreover, in the event of failure of a SACCO, people would be aware of their rights as members.

In summary, in their current form and scale, SACCOs won't work efficiently due to their large size, and people shouldn't be encouraged to join them. Those that exist with an inefficient size and structure for developmental reasons should be gradually divided into sub-groups of smaller sizes or transformed into larger, already regulated institutions.

Government regulation of SACCOs is a suboptimal solution. Instead, effective implementation of social capital through small, self-selected groups, proactive financial literacy efforts, and raising caution among members of SACCOs are ways to ensure effective governance of these groups.

Note: A previous version of this article was originally published on October 16, 2012 in The Daily Monitor, *a national newspaper in Uganda.*

Enhancing Uganda's Business Competitiveness

Every year, the World Economic Forum publishes the Global Competitiveness Index (GCI) Rankings, a comprehensive ranking of 144 countries based on micro- and macroeconomic factors of each country's competitiveness. In 2014/2015, Uganda ranked 122st on the GCI.[21] The country performed well with regard to labour market efficiency and the macroeconomic environment. However, on metrics such as infrastructure, higher education and training, and innovation, Uganda has much room for progress.

Economic productivity and an environment conducive to innovation are two key pillars of business competitiveness. Undoubtedly, labour productivity and the productivity of businesses in Uganda are critical for making it competitive on the global stage. A more productive labour force enables production of better quality goods and services in larger quantities at lower costs.

---

[21] *World Economic Forum, Uganda's detailed results in the Global Competitiveness Report 2014-2015.*
(http://reports.weforum.org/global-competitiveness-report-2014-2015/economies/#economy=UGA)

With this in view, in 2006 the government launched the Competitiveness and Investment Climate Strategy (CICS)[22] to trigger productivity in the sectors of agriculture, manufacturing, services, and tourism.

Productivity gains can translate into economic benefits only when coupled with an environment conducive for innovation. The World Bank produces a ranking of the impact of regulation on ease of doing business in 185 countries each year. According to the June 2012 ranking, Uganda ranks 120th among the 185 countries surveyed, which represents a decline from the 119th position in the previous year.[23] This ranking indicates ample room for improvement in the business environment in Uganda.

What Can Be Done to Improve Uganda's Business Environment?

Uganda needs to act in these four key areas to improve its business environment: 1) institutional reform, 2) entrepreneurship, 3) innovation, and 4) inclusion of the informal sector.

Institutional Reform: First, the country would be wise to accomplish institutional reform as the basis for any sustained improvement in the business environment. Legal institutions,

---

[22] Progress report on the implementation of the Doing Business in Uganda reform memo 2009, March 2012, Ministry of Finance, Planning and Economic Development
[23] Doing Business Databank
(http://www.doingbusiness.org/data/exploreeconomies/uganda/)

including the laws, the regulatory framework, and the judicial system as well as legal professionals play a crucial role in creating an environment conducive to business.

Recognising this, the CICS secretariat has embarked on specific initiatives such as business licensing reform, prioritisation of the enactment of 26 commercial bills, and advocating for e-governance. A Doing Business Task Force with both public and private sector representatives will drive institutional reforms.[24]

In Singapore, the country that's been consistently ranked first in the World Bank's rankings, it takes merely three working days to register a business versus 33 in Uganda.[25] Therefore, a priority for Uganda needs to be simplifying its legal and regulatory procedures to close the gap in such measures.

Currently, four agencies are involved when starting a business in Uganda.[26] However, the e-governance initiative led by the CICS secretariat is expected to create a One Stop Shop. This will integrate business incorporation services with other business registration requirements. Such processes as tax registration, trade licensing, and social security registration will be available in one place, thus dramatically reducing the time for starting a business.

---

[24] Other partnerships also include the Presidential Investors Roundtable, the Private Sector Development Group, and regional networks.
[25] Doing Business Databank
(http://www.doingbusiness.org/data/exploreeconomies/singapore/)
[26] Uganda Registration Bureau Service, Uganda Revenue Authority, National Social Security Fund (NSSF), and the local government authority

Similarly, through the Uganda Investment Climate Program (UICP), an electronic registry for all valid business licenses in Uganda is being established whereby all relevant information and forms can be readily accessed.

Promotion of Entrepreneurship: Second, Uganda must develop an ecosystem that can promote entrepreneurship. Such an ecosystem would need: 1) a sound institutional environment, 2) funding for new ideas, 3) business training for aspiring entrepreneurs, 4) financial literacy, and 5) financial products catering to early-stage businesses.

All of this can't happen overnight. Such development requires an exchange of ideas and mentorship from entrepreneurs beyond country borders. For example, Chile has attempted this with Startup Chile,[27] a programme funded by the Chilean government for inviting the best and the brightest entrepreneurs from around the globe and embedding them in the entrepreneurial ecosystem in the country. Ghana partners with Carnegie Mellon University on technological innovations. Indonesia is transforming itself into a hub for entrepreneurship in South East Asia.

So having partnerships with institutions oriented toward entrepreneurship and entrepreneurs beyond the region are critical. Given that the resources of the Ugandan government are strained,

---

[27] Startup Chile website (http://www.startupchile.org/)

any government support should be considered complementary to such programs.

Innovation with Stability: The third key is that innovation needs to be balanced with stability. Business and financial innovations hold the promise of tremendous opportunity for businesses in Uganda. However, equally significant are the risks these innovations entail. Technological innovations, advances in payment systems, and other improvements related to financial access and taxation deserve special attention.

Innovations such as the previously mentioned One Stop Shop envisioned through the e-governance initiative will utilize information and communication technology to share critical information for businesses. This will avoid the requirement to submit the same information to different regulatory institutions. As a result, it will streamline regulatory requirements and facilitate business in Uganda.

I suggest regulating mobile money in the East African region is absolutely relevant. Bank of Uganda is taking a keen interest in this area for the protection of the users as well as for the stability of the financial system. For example, cross-border remittances through mobile phones can lower transaction costs both in terms of money and time. However, as soon as large business transactions occur over mobile phones, a highly vigilant anti-money-laundering process needs to be in place.

Innovations such as the establishment of the Credit Reference Bureau would encourage more competition and transparency of borrower information in the credit markets over time. BOU is also making efforts to increase the financial literacy and ease of access to finance through innovations such as agent banking, especially for individuals in rural areas and for small and medium enterprises (SMEs). It is exploring innovative mechanisms such as agent banking that can enable commercial banks to expand their reach.

The availability of sound, affordable financial products is indispensable for maintaining the competitiveness of Uganda's businesses. Under the Uganda Investment Climate Program, the SME tax regime is also being reformed with a 20% reduction in SME compliance costs.

Inclusion of the Informal Sector: Fourth, expanding the reach of Uganda's regulatory framework to include the informal sector is necessary to increase the stability of its businesses and the effectiveness of supporting mechanisms such as payment systems and the judicial system. Only when the informal sector is on a level playing field with the formal sector can the country tap into the full potential of domestic business in Uganda. From there, it can effectively mitigate any risks.

It's important to first bring the informal sector under the regulatory ambit before contracts with such businesses can be enforced by the judiciary. The Companies Bill No. 14 of 2009 provides for the incorporation of a One Person Company (OPC), which will encourage formalizing many informal businesses in Uganda. In 2012, the Companies Bill No. 14 of 2009 was passed into law and in July 2013, the statutory instrument bringing the Companies Act of 2012 into force was passed.[28]

Uganda has numerous opportunities for enhancing its business competitiveness, both in the region and globally. Creation of an environment conducive to business is vital for businesses to be able to harness these opportunities. Institutional reform, striking the right balance between innovation and stability, promoting entrepreneurship, and expanding the reach of policy to the informal sector are key areas of focus to enhance competitiveness.

Note on recent developments: A previous version of this article was originally published online on the blog Africa at LSE, on April 10, 2013. In the 2015/2016 Global Competitiveness Report corruption was cited as the most problematic factor for doing business in Uganda ahead of access to finance, taxation and the supply of infrastructure.

---

[28] Article by Sheilla Atim, a lawyer and popular blogger in Uganda (http://sheillokeny.blogspot.ca/2013/11/normal-0-false-false-false-en-us-x-none_11.html)